# YOUR KNOWLEDGE HAS VALUE

Junaid Javaid

# Corporate Social Responsibility & Corporate Financial Performance Relationship: Evidence from UK´s Food Industry

GRIN Verlag

**Bibliografische Information der Deutschen Nationalbibliothek:**

Die Deutsche Bibliothek verzeichnet diese Publikation in der Deutschen National-
bibliografie; detaillierte bibliografische Daten sind im Internet über http://dnb.d-
nb.de/ abrufbar.

**Imprint:**

Copyright © 2012 GRIN Verlag GmbH
Druck und Bindung: Books on Demand GmbH, Norderstedt Germany
ISBN: 978-3-656-74815-1

**This book at GRIN:**

http://www.grin.com/en/e-book/281112/corporate-social-responsibility-corporate-
financial-performance-relationship

**GRIN - Your knowledge has value**

Der GRIN Verlag publiziert seit 1998 wissenschaftliche Arbeiten von Studenten, Hochschullehrern und anderen Akademikern als eBook und gedrucktes Buch. Die Verlagswebsite www.grin.com ist die ideale Plattform zur Veröffentlichung von Hausarbeiten, Abschlussarbeiten, wissenschaftlichen Aufsätzen, Dissertationen und Fachbüchern.

**Visit us on the internet:**

http://www.grin.com/

http://www.facebook.com/grincom

http://www.twitter.com/grin_com

# CORPORATE SOCIAL RESPONSIBILITY (CSR) & CORPORATE FINANCIAL PERFORMANCE (CEP) RELATIONSHIP: EVIDENCE FROM THE UK's FOOD INDUSTRY

RESEARCH PLAN

CORPORATE FINANCE
ASSESSMENT- 1

INDIVIDUAL REPORT

WRITTEN & SUBMITTED BY:

JUNAID JAVAID

SUBMISSION DATE: 14[H] DECEMBER 2012

# Corporate Social Responsibility (CSR) Disclosure & Corporate Financial Performance (CFP) Relationship: Evidence from the UK's Food Industry

Research Plan

**Keywords: Corporate Social Responsibility (CSR), Corporate Financial Performance (CFP)**

## 1. Research Questions & Research Objectives

The main purpose of the proposed research paper will be to investigate the impact of Corporate Social Responsibility on the listed companies' share price in order to evaluate and analyse its contribution to their increases. In the below portion, the research questions with its objectives are listed and briefly discussed below:

### 1.1. Research Question

The Research Questions for the desired research paper are listed below:

- What Impact the Corporate Social Responsibility (CSR) Disclosure would made on the Corporate Financial Performance (CFP)?
- Is it any relationship exists between the firm's CSR and its performance based on its share prices.
- Identify at least one dimension of Corporate Social Responsibility (CSR) which would be positively related to Corporate Financial Performance (CFP)?
- Investigate and Presents the benefits of CSR's implementation to the UK's Food Industry financial and market performance?

So it is cleared that the questions are properly designed in order to accomplish the core objective of the Proposed Research Paper.

## 1.2. Research Objectives

The objectives of the proposed Research Paper are outlined below:

- To discover that either the CSR Disclosure is positive or negatively related to the Corporate Financial Performance.
- To learn that either the CSR based on environmental reporting resulting in increasing the listed companies' share prices or not.
- To identify at least one dimension of CSR disclosure which is positive significantly related to the Corporate Financial Performance (CFP), in order to direct the companies under discussion to focus and emphasis on that particular CSR's dimension.
- To understand the importance of CSR Disclosure and its implementation within the UK's Food Industry.

## 2. Research Methodology

The Research Methodology adopted for the proposed research will be based on the both approaches: quantitative approach as well as qualitative approach. The quantitative approach will be adopted and implemented for the first two questions as it involved the use and analysis of certain CSR and Financial measures. Whereas the last the question will be based on the qualitative approach it will involve the interview of several companies stakeholders (Investors, Stock Analysts and the Consumers). The brief description of these two approaches along with its measures is mentioned below.

### 2.1. Quantitative Approach

#### 2.1.1. Measurements of Corporate Social Responsibility (CSR)

For the purpose of measuring the CSR disclosure, this research study will adopt the methodology named as Disclosure Scoring, which would be based entirely on the technique called content analysis which incorporates and includes four important CSR indicators (Employee Retention, Community Involvement, Product and the Environment). Each factor then has more sub-item disclosure which needed to be adjusted and disclosed depending on the type of specified item disclosure. Al-Tuwaijri, et al. (2004) stated and proposed that the objective of underlined process can be achieved with the use of diclosure measures that uses quantitative approach by assigning and denoting weights to the different disclosure items depending on their importance in the within the given user category which will be marked and denoted as the greatest weight in order to quantify the disclosures items incorporated in the CSR indicator as mentioned above (Al-Tuwaijri, et al., 2004). So in this manner marking and assiging the next the item with less wieght than the previous one. So as the item included in the disclore measures will receive the minimum wieght. It has also being elaborated that the firm which failed to disclose the any of the information on the defined indicators will be managed receive zero score. So this research will adop and utilise this above procedures for the purpose of measuring Corporate Social Responsibility (CSR) Diclosure.

### 2.1.2. Measurements of Financial Performance

The proposed research paper will use three identical financial measure of performance which will be determined as the dependent variables for the given research. All of these measure comes under the umbrella of accounting based performance measure which are listed and explained below:

#### 2.1.2.1. Return on Assets (ROA)

The main reason for using this performance measure as dependent variable is due its reliability and importance in accounting term as it is predicted to be less manipulated and is used widely to widely to measure the corporation's financial performance over a time period (Yoshikawa & Phan, 2003).

#### 2.1.2.2. Stock Market Return (R$_i$)

The reason for using this performance measure as dependent variable is that the investor's behaviour as now a day investors are more conscious and emphasized towards the stock return (Yoshikawa & Phan, 2003).

#### 2.1.2.3. Tobin's q ratio

The reasons for using Tobin's q ratio is due to the current trend as financial performance measures has became widespread in Empirical market analysis. And now it is the widely used financial performance measure, which is calculated by dividing the value of underlying firm with its asset's replacement cost (Hirsch & Seaks, 1993). It is important to illustrate more that the Tobin's q ratio is also termed as crucial for testing reported results' robustness which is the alternative measure of financial performance (Welch, 2003). The Tobin's q ratio is basically a representation of certain community of investors which are to be constrained or doubt by the businesses insight (Demsetz & Villalonga, 2001).

So, it has been demonstrated that on the basis of this research paper objectives, these all variables will be used and adopted on respective manner, In short, it has been cleared and understood that three variables (Return on Assets, Stock Market Return and Tobin's q ration) will be used as dependent variables. Whereas the for the purpose making findings and conclusion, four Corporate Social Responsibility (CSR) Disclosure measures (Employee's Relational Dimension, Environmental Dimension, Product Dimension and Community Involvement Dimension) will be used as Independent variable for the desired research study. These both measures (Performance & CSR Disclosure) together will able to the control the effect on certain variables listed below:

a) System Risk (BETA)
b) Financial Leverage (LEV)
c) Company's size (SIZE)
d) Company's turnover (SALES)
e) Company's asset turnover (ATR)
f) Earnings Per Share (EPS)

## 2.2. Qualitative Approach

### 2.2.1. Interview

For the purpose of researching through the fourth and the last question, certain interviews will be conducted. These interviews will be based on the Qualitative Approach in which companies' stakeholders (Investors, Stock Analysts and Consumers) will be the main participants. This purpose of this qualitative approach will be to determine the importance of CSR Disclosure implementation in UK's Food Industry. The discussion involved in this method will be preceded in three parts. The first phase will be designed to assess the participant's understanding CSR disclosure. The second part will be based on the factors which will directly affects the participant's investing behaviour. And the last section will be made on the perspective which will evaluate the affect of CSR Disclosure on the participant's investing decision.

So in this manner, the Research Methodology will be perfectly aligned with the Research paper's problem statements and also with its objectives which must be accomplished for the making the proposed research paper more authentic and more reliable which would be used as a contributing factor for the future piece of work conducted in this field.

## 3. Literature Review

The proposed research paper will be made on perspective of Corporate Social Responsibility Disclosure so in this regard all the Literature will carefully be analysed and reviews in order to address the research questions. Hence the section of Literature Review will be focused on certain points mentioned below:

- Providing and illustrating background information on CSR disclosure measures and Financial performance measures in order to elaborate reasons of choosing both measures as independent and dependent variable.

- Define certain dimensions of CSR measures to identify their respective impact on given Corporate Financial Performance (CFP) measures.

- Making a list of CSR disclosure dimensions which could contribute a lot in increasing the company's share price which then make direct impact on the CFP measures and therefore resulted in maximising shareholders value.

In addition to the above points, certain empirical studies on the Linkage between Corporate Social Responsibility (CSR) and Corporate Financial Performance (CFP) will carefully be assessed, the description of these studies are briefly discussed below:

### 3.1. Empirical Studies on Finding the Relationship between CSR and CFP

The empirical studies on the linkage of CSR and CFP were started to develop about three decades ago and the majority of the Literature was proposed by the western countries. The Literature on the relationship of CSR and CFP is basically divided in to two types of empirical study. The first set had used the methodology to estimate the impact of company's engagement in Corporate Social Act on its short-term financial performance measures in term of abnormal rate of return (Hannon & Milkovich, 1996;

6

Wright & Ferris, 1997; Posnikoff, 1997; McWilliams & Siegel, 2001). The results of all those studies were of mixed nature. as the findings of Wright & Ferris (1997) was suggested a negative correlation, whereas Posnikoff (1997) illustrated postive relationship between CSR and CFP. The study of McWilliams & Siegel (2001) resulted in raising some issues and concerns on the CSR and the CFP short-run results.

The second set of studies examined the realtionship intensity between CSR disclosure measures and CFP long-term measures such as profitability over a specified period of time (Aupperle, et al., 1985; Sundgren & Schneeweis, 1988; Waddock & Graves, 1997; Simpson & Kohers, 2002; Mahoney & Roberts, 2007). Like the previous set, this set also generated mixed result, Aupperle, et al. (1985) found out that there is no relationship exists between CSR disclosure and performance measure (profitability) on the other side Sundgren & Schneeweis (1988) depicted that CSR disclosure measures and the long term profitability measures are closely related to each other. And in the end Simpson & Kohers (2002) and Waddock & Graves (1997) found out significantly strong relationship between prior measures and also shown some CSR dimensions which can have direct  influence of firm's long term profitability and this could be sustained over a long span of time.

Allthough the above studies were mostly carried out in US and UK  market settings. The research on Asian companies' CSR disclosure and CFP relationship was conducted by Subroto (2002). For this purpose he emphasized more on the explanatory survey and used statistical measuremet method called Multivariate Correlations and also based his research on the cross-sectional data. The most important for od this research study was the analysis og the correlation between CSR disclosure and CFP which would directly made an impact on Indonesian Business practices. In that study study three hypothesis were tested. The findings from the first hypothesis  shown the significant interest of all stakeholders rowards the CSR disclosre, whereas the seconf hypothesis result elaborated that all stakeholders are more enthusiastic towards knowing about the CSR diclosure contribution its corporation's financial performance. The result of the last hypothesis recommends that there is a quite low level of correlation exists between the Asian companies' CSR disclosure and their CFP measures. So the result of this study suggest that only the western countries corporations are more aggressive in disclosing its CSR dusclosure and this is the reason why it is sometime really hard to find Asian listed corporation's environmental reports as they regret its effects on the given corporation profitability which is directly related to the compsnies financial performance measures which will be used for this proposed research paper.

## 4. Data Sources

For the proposed research paper the industry which would be selected is the UK's Food Industry. And in this regard 65 companies in the relevant industry which are listed on the London Stock Exchange will carefully be analysed to draw the final result. The reason for going for this industry is because of its nature and characteristics (Concentrated and Intense Rivalry) which is also categorized under UK's high profile industry. This was main reason the this industry selection as it has been assumed that the companies engaging in high profile industry are more likely to report and disclose more information on its CSR measures with an intention of changing deflecting attentions, public expectation and perceptions (Cuganesan, et al., 2007).

In relation to answer research question-2, the data on the UK's food Industry Companies' share prices will be collected from the UK Yahoo Finance Website. The companies' share price data will collected for the time period of 5 years (2000-2005) and share prices will be collected on the monthly based so it means that total 60 figures of data will be collected to accomplish the objective associated with the given research question. The reason for choosing the given time span is that it was a period of recovery from the financial crisis which hit all countries of the world and also the time of emergence of capital markets, whereas the second reason was proposing this time period for the desired research is that at that time the Corporate Social Responsibility disclosure practices was at its infancy stage.

In relation to answer research question 1 & 3, data on two quantitative measures (CFP and CSR) will be collected. For the purpose of finding the each company financial performance measures (Return on Assets, Stock Market Return and Tobin's q ration) data, the Website called businessweek.com will used to collected the financial performance measures figures from the given time period on the quarterly basis in to make the desired research and result more accurate and more reliable.

For the purpose of collecting data on CSR disclosure measures (Employee's Relational Dimension, Environmental Dimension, Product Dimension and Community Involvement Dimension), data willed collected from the selected companies' annual report which can be downloaded from the respective companies' websites or from the Bank of England Website. So the collection of data on CSR disclosure will be the great deal as it involves the process of going the companies annual as it is also be considered as the biggest source of collecting and analyzing corporate environmental reporting information. Further it is important to mention that the designated source of information on Annual reports can be accessible in form of electronic formats or hardcopies.

To answer the research question 4, the questionnaire has to be designed and prepared which would reflect the true picture of its objectives and should be made in a format which can be easily understood by the stakeholders to be questioned to reach the final conclusion.

So from the above portion it has been cleared that the both data sources (Primary and Secondary) will be used and which will be based on both approaches (Qualitative & Quantitative) in order to make and reach towards final decision.

## 5. Possible Problems

In order to conduct the research study on finding the relationship between the UK's Food Industry Corporate Social Responsibility (CSR) and Corporate Financial Performance (CFP) which based mainly on the companies dealing the respective industry share price movements, one would expose to several problems which are briefly outlined below:

### 5.1. Research Proposal Rejection

As it is already understood that before conducting any research,, it has to be accepted by the supervisor by the submitting the research problem on the given topic. In this regard, my topic is relating to identify the desired relationship between the CSR Disclosure measures and CFP measures within the UK's food industry. So I have to consult the Literature Review on the proposed relationship in depth in order to come up with certain Research Question and Research Objective which would be determined as the contributing factor in the present literature on these measures and also on their relationship.

## 5.2. Data Unreliability Factor in Conducting Survey

As it has already mentioned that the proposed research paper's fourth question is closely with the Qualitative Approach for which the questionnaire would needed to prepared for the purpose of collecting first hand data. The participants who would be approached for this purpose are the stakeholders (Stock Analysts, Investors and Consumers). It has to keep one thing in mind that not all audience member would answer the questions in true context which would be resulted in executing the alpha-test value of questionnaire within the range of being categorized as the unreliable data which would also make negative impact on the selected research instrument (Questionnaire). So in order to get rid of this problem I must have to conduct survey on the more questionnaire from the selected range (100) in order to remove certain questionnaire from the approved ones, if I will have doubt on some questionnaire's reliability and its context (not honestly completed).

## 5.3. Failed to Collected information on CSR Disclosure Measures

As I already mentioned that the information on CSR Disclosure measures will be most to collect as it involved the process of going through the selected Companies within UK's Food Industry Annual reports. So there would be many chances that I would not able to collect the data which I'm wished for, as the pro-forma of all companies environmental reporting varies from each other. In order to resolve this issue I would have to make myself clear of the fact that I would have to explore some companies' annual report in Hard copies format. And also will have to study Al-Tuwaijri, et al. (2004) in detaiils as the procedure which would be followed is briefly discussed in this research study. So in this manner, I will not only able to identify CSR disclosure measures accurately but also be remained away from that predicted problem.

## 5.4. Failed to generate interpret Results

Although. I have the knowledge of using statistical software called SPSS. But I would faced the problem of generating and interpreting as I used this software a year ago. So in order for reflecting the originality and reliability of collected data I will have to attend some classes on the SPSS tutorial in order to overcome the potential which would make heavy influence on the selected research study. And I also needed to remain conscious and attentive during the data entry process as even one wrong figure could manipulate the whole procedure which would leaded towards outlining the wrong result.

## 6. Milestones of Proposed Research

The Gant Chart for the conducting of the proposed research paper is listed below along with its table:

| Milestones | Start Date | Duration | End Date |
|---|---|---|---|
| Research Questions & Research Objectives | 1-Jan-13 | 9 | 10-Jan-13 |
| Literature Review | 10-Jan-13 | 24 | 3-Feb-13 |
| Research Methodology | 10-Feb-13 | 10 | 20-Feb-13 |
| Collecting Data on Share Prices | 20-Feb-13 | 9 | 1-Mar-13 |
| Collecting Data on Financial Performance Measures | 2-Mar-13 | 8 | 10-Mar-13 |
| Collecting Data on Companies Environmental Reporting | 10-Mar-13 | 16 | 26-Mar-13 |
| Creating Questionaire | 26-Mar-13 | 10 | 5-Apr-13 |
| Conducting Survey | 6-Apr-13 | 18 | 24-Apr-13 |
| Entering Data into SPSS | 25-Apr-13 | 10 | 5-May-13 |
| Generating Results | 5-May-13 | 5 | 10-May-13 |
| Interpretating Results | 10-May-13 | 15 | 25-May-13 |
| Formulating Findings, Discussion & Concusion | 25-May-13 | 11 | 5-Jun-13 |
| Generate Reference List | 6-Jun-13 | 4 | 10-Jun-13 |
| Format the Research Paper according to the Journal of Accounting & Finance Proforma | 11-Jun-13 | 9 | 20-Jun-13 |

Table 1 Milestones' Table

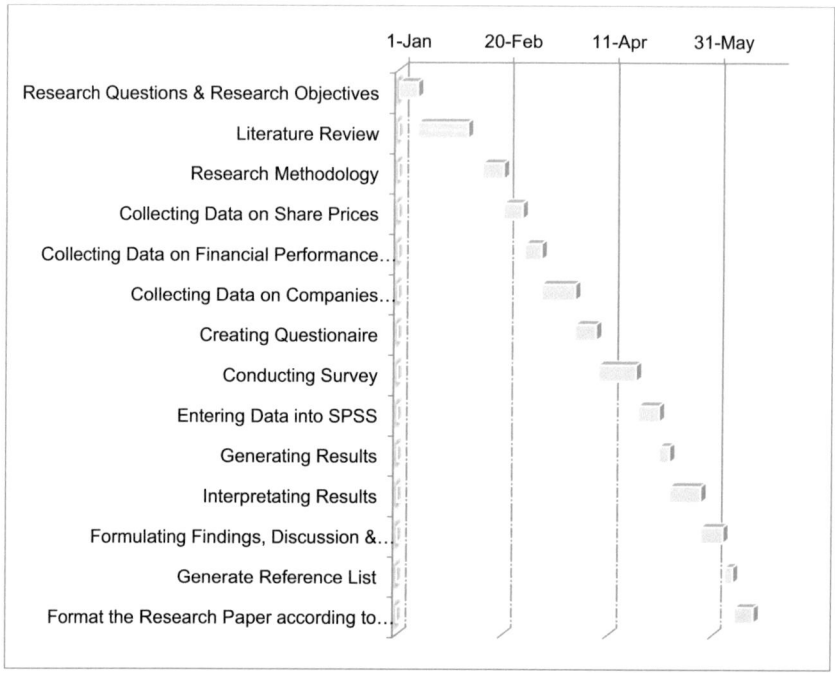

Figure 1 Gantt Chart for Porposed Research Paper

## 7. References

Al-Tuwaijri, S., Christensen, T. & Hughes, K., 2004. The relations among
environmental disclosure, environmental performance, and economic performance:
A simultaneous equations approach. *Accounting, Organizations and Society,* Volume
29, pp. 447-471.

Aupperle, K., Carroll, A. & Hatfield, J., 1985. An empirical examination of the
relationship between corporate social responsibility and profitability. *Academy of
Management Journal,* 28(2), pp. 446-463.

Cuganesan, S., Ward, L. & Guthrie, J., 2007. *Legitimacy Theory: A Story of
Reporting Social and Environmental Matters within the Australian Food and
Beverage Industry,* Auckland: Asian Pacific Interdisciplinary Research in Accounting
(APIRA).

Demsetz, H. & Villalonga, B., 2001. Ownership structure and corporate performance.
*Journal of Corporate Finance,* 7(3), pp. 209-333.

Hannon, J. & Milkovich, G., 1996. The effect of human resource reputation signals on share prices: An event study. Human Resource Management. 35(3), pp. 405-424.

Hirsch, B. & Seaks, T., 1993. Functional form in regression models of Tobin's q. Review of Economics and Statistics, 75(2), pp. 381-386.

Mahoney, L. & Roberts, R., 2007. Corporate social performance, and financial performance and institutional ownership in Canadian firms. Accounting Forum, Volume 31, pp. 233-253.

McWilliams, A. & Siegel, D., 2001. Corporate social responsibility: a theory of the firm perspective. Academy of Management Review, 26(1), pp. 117-127.

Posnikoff, J. F., 1997. Disinvestment from South Africa: They did well by doing good. Contemporary Economic Policy. 15(1), pp. 76-86.

Simpson, W. & Kohers, T., 2002. The link between corporate social and financial performance: Evidence from the banking industry. Journal of Business Ethics, Volume 35, pp. 97-109.

Subroto, P. H., 2002. A correlational study of corporate social responsibility and financial performance: an empirical survey toward ethical business practices in Indonesia., Jakarta: Capella University.

Sundgren, A. & Schneeweis, T., 1988. Corporate social responsibility and firm financial performance. Academy of Management Journal, 31(4), pp. 854-872.

Waddock, S. & Graves, S., 1997. The corporate social performance-financial performance link. Strategic Management Journal, Volume 18, pp. 303-319.

Welch, E., 2003. The Relationship between Ownership Structure and Performance in Listed Australian Companies. Australian Journal of Management, Volume 28, pp. 287-305.

Wright, P. & Ferris, S., 1997. Agency conflict and corporate strategy: Effect of divestment on corporate value. Strategic Management Journal, 18(1), pp. 77-83.

Yoshikawa, T. & Phan, P., 2003. The performance implications of ownership-driven governance reform. European Management Journal, 21(6), pp. 698-506.